I0791428

FROM A CATERPILLAR
TO
A BUTTERFLY

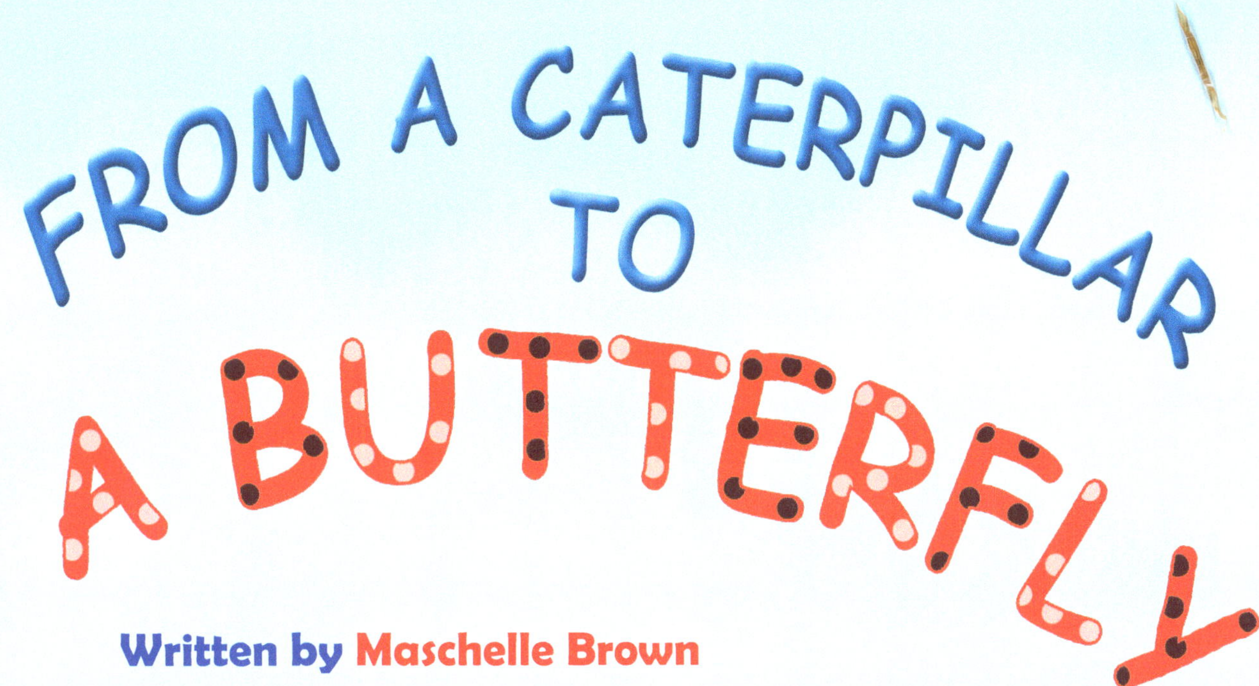

Written by **Maschelle Brown**

Illustrated by **Funda Girgin**

BUTTERFLIES

Butterflies are beautiful just like humans. There are many species or types of butterflies. Just like humans, every butterfly is a little different. Even though some butterflies are the same species they may not look alike.

A BUTTERFLY'S LIFE CYCLE

Every butterfly has four stages of life.

1. EGG
2. CATERPILLAR
3. PUPA OR CHRYSALIS
4. ADULT OR FLIGHT PERIOD

EGG

Butterflie's eggs have different architecture or shapes. Some species lay a single egg while other species lay lots of eggs. The butterfly eggs take four (4) days to hatch into a caterpillar. Eggs are very important in a butterfly's life cycle.

CATERPILLAR

Caterpillars are like babies. The only job of a caterpillar is to eat and grow just like babies. Sometimes a caterpillar grows too big, then it has to shed its old skin. This is called the WINSTAR stage. A caterpillar will eat the plants in your garden.

PUPA or CHRYSALIS

The caterpillar is now sleeping in a hard shell (chrysalis or cocoon). This is the miracle stage, one of the beauties and mysteries of a butterfly. Inside the chrysalis the transformation takes place.

After two weeks the caterpillar now changes into the body of a beautiful butterfly.

ADULT BUTTERFLY AND THEIR CONDUCT

A fully formed adult butterfly breaks from the pupa with its wing still folded. Butterflies are smart and love warm weather. Butterflies lay their eggs and look for their mates on the same plants caterpillars eat. Butterflies feed from plants with nectar like bees.

The main duty of an adult butterfly
is to find a mate, reproduce and
continue THE BEAUTIFUL BUTTERFLY
LIFE CYCLE.

MYTHS, FACTS AND BUTTERFLIES

The butterfly in many cultures represents change, growth, renewal and resurrection. Some Native Americans see butterflies as joy colors and change.
Butterflies represent the soul in many past cultures. "Psyche" means soul. It is a Greek word often associated with butterflies.

Butterflies live on all liquid diet.
A Butterfly waits 2 hours for their body to get hard and for liquids to circulate in their wings before they can fly.